Social Media Success How To Become An Influencer

SADANAND PUJARI

Published by SADANAND PUJARI, 2023.

Table of Contents

Copyright 1

About.. 2

Introduction.. 3

What is Influencer Marketing ? 5

Choose Your Niche 7

What It is & How It Works..11

Getting A Business Account......................................14

Consistency is Key...17

Using the Right Hashtags 20

Writing Captions 23

Analyze Your Audience 26

Connect with Influencers...29

Interact with Followers...32

Contact Brands 35

Building Your Profile...38

Just Be Yourself..42

Set Your Goals 45

Be Consistent...48

Analyze Your Data	50
Contact Brands	53
What It is & How It Works	57
Get a Pro Account	59
Videos You Should Create	62
Your Tik Tok Strategy	64
Getting More Followers	66
Followers Hack : Challenges	68
Post Frequently	71
Using Tik Tok Analytics	73
When to Contact Brands	76
Conclusion	79

Copyright

Copyright © 2023 by **SADANAND PUJARI**

All rights reserved. No part of this book may be reproduced, scanned, or distributed in any printed or electronic form without permission. Please do not participate in or encourage piracy of copyrighted materials in violation of the author's rights. Purchase only authorized editions.

Social Media Success How To Become An Influencer

First Edition: Dec 2023

Book Design by **SADANAND PUJARI**

About

Influencer Marketing is a really powerful form of advertising that you can learn to use quickly and easily. It's not complicated. It takes no high-tech talent, or math degree to figure out. You just work with nice people - and they promote your products.

The truth is - Getting Facebook Ads to actually convert at a level that is worth the money you spend on them is really hard. Most Facebook Advertisers waste all their money - and don't have anything to show for it. It's not your fault. It's a system that has a very low probability of success. Stop the madness.

Everyone can learn Influencer marketing. It's much easier than complicated paid ad platforms.

We'd love to have you jump into this masterclass and learn how to solve your traffic problems with Influencer Marketing!

Introduction

Marketing as well as technology has evolved, potentially in recent years, more seems to have emerged, giving rise to new strategies that help brands, companies or organizations to achieve their objectives, which in most cases consist of greater exposure, recognition and obviously a higher number of sales. Social network. While the product of evolution 'is very essential purpose is based on connection because they were initially intended for that purpose to connect us with other people anywhere in the world faced with such a possibility.

Brands have entered this world by putting millions of goods and the service within each of the customers with just a click or tap on the screen of your smartphone. This trend gave rise to competition, that is, since most brands organizations draw on the word of social media. And what would differentiate them, the answer is simple strategies. They decide. To apply to reach their customers today, the pace of their life has changed.

Compare it to that of a decade ago. Today, people got dazzling speed. So the use of traditional marketing has become obsolete for many brands giving away to the purpose of digital marketing, which is nothing more than moving the strategies of adapting them to digital playing.

We will mention many digital marketing strategies that have been the result of numerous studies in recent years and even say that there are as many ways to apply them as creativity allows. However, on this occasion we will emphasize one of the most effective ways in this Book, especially if this is a matter of increasing the exposure and scope of any product influencer marketing.

What is Influencer Marketing ?

But what is the influence or marketing influence or marketing is a new digital marketing strategy that consists of achieving a series of collaborative links between brands and companies and those people with high visibility and prominence on the Internet known as influencers. So one of the influencers are not superhuman or magical creatures that hold the secret of social networks, you know, magical books.

Do you have people who are simply characterized by having a lot of receptivity and charisma in the virtual world? Some of them, like YouTube, for example, have channels with the Saudis and in some cases even millions of subscribers and followers. Influencers play a role as a product of a technological evolution which plays a critical role in today's life. Naturally, this social networking site on real DIMOS in Europe for brands, companies and organization, even entrepreneurs with emerging businesses, this critique of a specific a product or their appearance using a brand of clothing, for instance, are considerably increasing the widespread acceptance of a specific brand and therefore boosting sales like a phone for companies.

Applying this strategy can bring a significant benefit, some as follows you can to amplify the positive message of the brand or company. You will generate a lot of conversation on the net about the product over by Deben. It increases traffic to the website or social media social network profile of the brand. The influencer is promoting the brand that gains a good reputation and the high percentage if designed well. A campaign with influencers does not have to be expensive, and it can yield a satisfactory and a profitable return on the investment.

Influencers are generally followed by a target audience characterized for being very consumerist, having a high purchase power billion dollars but becoming an influencer and being considered an influencer is not only about having many followers, it's about hiding our opinion followed and then considered by a particular audience. And at the same time, this implies a lot of hard work. That involves a lot of learning, perseverance and dedication to being a successful influencer. You must not only know how to use leading social networks, much less.

How to make a beautiful publication is a role considered a profession that you must take very seriously. If you want to be considered by the biggest brand in the market, if you wish to be successful. We do not have a magical formula, but we have prepared this Book with some secrets. They will surely change your perspective and to guide you in the process of becoming an influencer.

Choose Your Niche

There is no magic formula to become a recognized influencer, however, you will need a charm to please your followers and to be always at the forefront of the trends, because in the digital world, the last thing you want is to lag. But there are secrets you can start using to stand out while they are to target a specific niche. In other words, to stand out, you must find a target audience to address.

And to do that you must talk to them about a specific topic, something you stand out in a unique way and in a way that makes you stand out from the rest. It doesn't matter if you have 1000 or 100000 followers. Would this ensure that by speaking to a group for specific in each particular topic, you will achieve an audience that is highly committed to your content, this commitment that will ultimately translate not only into followers, but consumers of your content and the audience that is loyal to you and Of course, trust your judgment.

Also, it will undoubtedly make brands want to approach you eager to reach an audience, and commit it to your criteria. So how do you choose a niche? The answer will depend on you and your skills because if you are strong in the kitchen, you cannot target an audience that loves fashion design or choose a niche in the manufacture of summer clothes. Does this mean you should stick to only one scene? Not exactly. Everything is on its own time in social networks. There are millions of people who have a great deal of content and target different audiences. Other work. There is something for everyone.

Choosing a niche is a task that requires time and planning, especially if you intend to stand out amongst so many people who may be doing the same as you. So how can you choose a niche and now dying trying to do this? You must start by writing down a straightforward release with all the things that interest you and put special emphasis into those topics of your interest, the best that suits you or those that you want to display in your social network. Probably you will find that the rent on ptosis is enormous. Do you worry so much?

Don't worry so much about it. We will narrow down the options. So you are sort of later on. This works now. Pay attention to the following explanation. Focus on a niche. By now you should have written down all your interests and skills. These can be turned into niches. Some niche is a trendy and social network which stand out like fashion, art, travel, food, geek Capo's, Nyjer Babies, gamer's makeups, comedy photography and fitness, for example.

Let's say you like the fashion niche very much. However, this niche is extensive but is self. Therefore, whatever continent you post in your social network of choice may not be of sophisticated and the like the impact you want because it would be too general and diffuse to send out as a general. As fashion is, you can select something with even narrower options unless we get ourselves used to thinking outside the box following the example with the fashion needs. We have found various topics such as garment making, fashion blogging, fashion design, and fashion trends. You can also meet our needs even more.

For example, if you are a fashion designer, just being one and talking about it won't suffice. You can be even more specific about talking about making swimsuits for this idea. You can talk about making swimsuits only for ladies and only for men. So if you feel you have chosen a broad niche, you can go even deeper and adopt a smaller one. As you can see, making the surroundings look half of what you want to give to your followers and the subscribers is worth it says they'll have to know they will fund a specific and unique content in your site. Therefore, it's up to you to be as specific as possible and aim for an audience.

Another essential step to success. Our social network is not who you want to target for this task. You can look for inspiration. Other accounts targeting the same niche as you are completely valid. If you choose to aim for a similar style of the accounts, you look up for inspiration. It's not about copying them, but about being inspired by them. These are inspired as acidic that will help you identify yourself to an audience similar to Jersey. And in turn, have you found a similar follower base? Study your inspirational accounts carefully and fund your most. Successful policies and try to break them down into their core elements, this and that will help you generate a similar post.

Everything works as long as it's with your personal touch in the front of your originality, evaluated according to your content, what would be your ideal audience? That is, if what you like to do is to show you creative process. As a fashion designer, you cannot aim at a gamer audience. Choose a leading social network. Last but at the same time, the most crucial step through the network which you want to establish yourself. This doesn't mean that you have to choose to open an account in only one network and only dedicate yourself to it. No, but you should start in one initially, at least, while you consolidate your content and the black community. There are many networks where you can create content.

For example, Instagram, Facebook, Twitter and other most popular. However, YouTube can grant you quick fame if you use it correctly. Tip top and from the last few years became the most downloaded social network in most places, or an iPhone store to choose a social network to work on. You first need to know it, know how it works and why not. If secret, this knowledge will also help you fund a network that identifies with you.

For example, it's not safe to upload an image to Instagram, accompanied by a caption that makes you fall in love and to seduce the customer is not the same as making a video for YouTube that engages the subscriber enough to see the hosting. The Beisel resource to exploit your full potential is to understand which social network you want to be and to make the most of it.

To mostly use a network intranet is entrenched and the girl's Instagram, YouTube and time. However, this does not imply that other social networks are losing relevance still and will be very advisable to focus on the place where there is a higher number of people. Therefore, these are three networks the perfect target to become an influencer and to be the target of most recognizable brands.

What It is & How It Works

Instagram is a social platform based on mobile apps. It allows the user base to upload images and videos with multiple effects, such as stickers that filter the screen and then post them as content in the platform and share them across a wide array of social media. Initially, it was intended as a photographic work, since it was one of the first social networks that has a unique filter for photos. This allows the user to create a well added image and then give it a professional look without much effort anyone could add without using resources like Photoshop.

Instagram is coming into one of the leading social network platforms for both consumers and brands because they have more than 20 meaning influencers which work for the people as entertainers and opinion leaders and therefore brand as a promoter to generate the most sales to become an influencer within this robust social network in which there are more than one thousand meaning users a mouse. You have to be very charming to please your followers and always be at the forefront of trends in the digital world.

Would you want the least to be left behind on most social networks nowadays? Obviously the purpose of that is to humanize that social network more and more, since, according to experts in the last few years, social networks will become generators of social alienation. And in the face of such a concern, most social networks stick to an organism that consists of showing you what you like, taking you to those things with which you identify yourself and with which you interact the most.

A monster called Organism in 2018 and Instagram introduced menu changes to an operation such as a great operation that moved us away from the timeline with which we used to see pulses. But despite a worse reaction, the chronological presentation didn't seem to make a comeback. So it was up to each user to adapt and manage themselves under those new rules. Under these conditions, it is possible to adapt and overcome. The Instagram algorithm is the window to understand that the current hours and prioritize highly committed stories and poses communication by using different Instagram tools such as stories is something of value to the organism.

For this reason, resources like Instagram stories and Instagram TV will continue to evolve because in the social aspect of your marketing strategy on Instagram, from the very first transition of the timeline format, Instagram feeds become a scheme based primarily on interaction with other people's houses. These include the numbers like comments we do. We'll save forwarding, direct messaging and any other interaction the Post receives while posing as a lot of likes and comments. The aneurysms read it as a high quality post.

We engage in content and it's likely that most people will be interested in seeing a report about the new hour. Some Instagram representatives commented that the content already in your feed will depend on whether the algorithm determines the content as interesting for you and on the quality and quantity of interaction with a person who is posting. In other words, Instagram.

The operation is based on humanisation not looking to be robots, but the opposite Instagram. Seek to get closer to you by providing you with the tools that will allow you to get closer to your followers, get to know them and interact with them. It's up to you to do the job.

Getting A Business Account

The second thing to consider, if you want to be an Instagram influencer, is to take a serious hustle by converting your Instagram account to a business account. It doesn't matter if your account has already been created. You can change it from the switch to business account or switch to a greater account option on the setting tab. Or you can simply create a new account visa option, activate. These troops are already there and then you just have to use it.

What is the difference between a business and a greater account? With both options, you get almost the same to whoever the business account was created. Considering that in the last years numerous brands and a company has drawn the social this recently to the Greater Acasti. Why is the thinking that the high number of influencers that make life in this social network and that in turn dedicate a significant part of their time to create valuable content that keeps the followers hooked on the consumption much longer?

Accounts have been special, highly designed for influencers, allowing them to promote a good or service using their intimate knowledge. This option even allows you to label your sponsor enabling the creation of purely commercial content where the brand or the company gets advertised to 100 percent, while the knowledge he brought about by the creation will create her account. And another notable difference concerning the business is that the creator was originally the only one to allow you to visualize how many people stopped following you.

Nowadays, both options enable you to make it visible. However, both are a powerful Instagram tool that allows you to view your profile statistics if you want to be successful on these social networks. Now, we're creating a strategy based on these statistics. We become your ace in the hole in both options as a company is gramme or as a creator you can make an announcement this possible. I will undoubtedly be your greatest creative ally and unsubtly. Instagram options are free. The ads generate an expense that you must pay Mousley to Instagram based on the amount of advertising you do.

However, more than that expense is an investment that is one hundred percent worthwhile because it allows you to modify your reach and then by segmenting it in the right way, it will be a formula that will guarantee you to gain followers. Remember that just a company has a buyer, person and influencer. Much must have a target audience. So the way to make ads must be in conjunction with a brand. For this reason, Instagram, which is continuously involved, has provided its influencers with a new possibility for working with brands creating brand content, which means that creating ads for influencers brand the content is an evolving ecosystem.

So Instagram has been concerned with listening to the requests it receives from brands and influencers about a concentration of branded content and the influencer needs to know all the tools available to work with the brands. And this new possibility of creating ads is no exception. With this new functionality, brands will pay for advertising on Instagram down for the influencers advertising account. The expression is a breakthrough not only for brands, who will be able to control the metrics on the spot, but also for users who will now be able to know if the image they seek of an influencer with a casual look is commission or not.

How to configure branded content at step one first step. Assess the permissions approval for the branded content. The brand must gren the content creators permission to label the company its publication with a branded content. How this could be done. The brand must go to a wider profile in the Instagram app, select the options above the additive profile button and the truth of business setting. If the request or approval option is on, the approved accounts section will be displayed and if the option is off, you won't have to complete any more steps.

You must approve the account and add an Instagram user of the crater you are collaborating with to finally select. Then when you make a publication it is branded a countdown in the Instagram feed and the tag of the company you will see the option that says allow trading parties to promote publication when it's selected. I won't permit you to promote your branded organic effet posting ads that are an advertisement step to campaign set up ad manager when Ukraina ad for the.

Rendina condom publication Instagram, you can use a goal of reach for brand recognition, video playback traffic or interaction. The secret to advertising is beauty. Well segmented come in with an engaging image, a subjective caption and ending with a call to action. That leaves the audience wanting more from you, taking them to your profile where they follow you and get hooked on your contact.

Consistency is Key

Great and impeccable Instagram bio, his biography is Your Business Card, especially if would be an influencer has become your full time profession. It's a small box at the top of your profile so you can fill in with 150 characters defining who you are, what you do and why you should be followed. You should also come with a profile photo where your face is visible so that it's clear who you are.

Ideally, you should choose your best photo preferrable with a proper resolution so that it looks attractive. If you do not have a well-defined about graphy, you will not attract the attention of the people who target your profile. This can be an honor to use alternate useful words because you direct the public's attention to your profile, but fail to give them a good reason why they should stay.

The most important thing is that within your biography, you can add the most essential item that defines you, because in the end those details will be the ones that make a difference from the other memories. And what you want is to inspire confidence. And Of course, those who go to your profile will follow you and become part of your community. You must not forget to leave in your profile the link to your website or a particular page that you want them to see.

This will be the only place where they can click and to be really to hate. Even in influencer marketing this option is handy because it is a brand who wants to influence direct your audience to a specific link. They can leave it there and the influencer will work its magic by sending the audience to click on the link post regularly. Stay consistent. If you want to be successful, the secret will be the consistency with which you create content. And this is not just true for Instagram is right for any task you decide to undertake.

His Instagram is a network that continuously adapts to change and continuously updates. And the tools that flutter cumulated is a digital platform. If you want to be a successful Instagram influencer, keep an eye on the updates and trends. To do this, you must keep posting regularly. For example, the stories are excellent tools for better use, even if you decide not to post some days are valid but do not disappear. You can continue to keep your followers aware of your day by posting in your stories. Remember that Instagram seeks to humanize the social network and the values spontaneity to sort of stories do not necessarily require a large production.

Being consistent is not about posting too much, it is rather about creating quality content. Number three consistency plus the quality content is equal to guaranteed followers. Being consistent will allow you to take advantage of the new tools and the general interaction with. Remember, with every update, Instagram tells you what it likes and what your fans are likely to like. From a practical standpoint, if I were making a post that has all the necessary ingredients to generate a significant interaction, ideally you will maintain the standard and even succeed. That is, you must evaluate what your followers like and to keep them engaged with your post. The quality must also be consistent to do this in a more organized way.

You can create a posting calendar for this. You can use applications such as a plan only preview app Garney or even Google Calendar. A calendar will allow you to keep a specific order and not be left blank with nothing to post. It is best to take one day a week to organize the content you will post as long as you have the flexibility to allow for offsite posting if necessary. The magic begins when you develop a habit, then everything else is easier to do. If you can't discipline yourself to be consistent, you can sit down and spend time on the project whenever you want. You need to even have a little time. Discipline is a key to making the machine precise and easy to flow. In other words, constancy generates constancy.

Using the Right Hashtags

Although this application was brewing in 2010, in 2011, these already famous hashtags were added to happy user fun that you made use of the same subject, Instagram allows for certain hashtags per pulse. But what are the famous hashtags? Hashtags are words or phrases set in a hash sign with no spaces or special characters. They were like what was happening in. Their main objective is to segment the content that is published. So, for example, if you use a lab hashtag for several posts, whenever you click on that, you will see those same posts, plus others from public accounts that have the same hashtag to find the poses with a specific hashtag.

You can also use a magnifying glass at the bottom pole, too. If your goal is a ground group, a certain number of pulses using a hashtag will help you lead the public to those particular posts. Usually hashtags go with a caption that can be either short or medium long. The hashtags you write can be about almost anything as you type in Instagram, which suggests text based on their popularity. Tectonically, you can use up to 30 each post. Why is it essential to use hashtags on Instagram? There are three main advantages of using hashtags, probably on social networks.

Hashtags allow users to fund your posts quickly and to help them go viral. By increasing visibility, you increase the reach of their message and increase the number of followers of their brand on Instagram. There's a direct link between hashtags and engagement to more hashtags that you use and more visibility of your publication if and the more likely people will interact with you. How do I use hashtags in Israel? There are some recommendations to keep in line focused on the goal before defining your project. Research will hashtag so your competition, your followers and industry influencers use hashtags as keywords.

For example, if your niche is interior design hashtags like a room deck or room inspiration or attract people seeking inspiration for their rooms, use hashtag search engines to identify the words that are closest to your audience using popular hashtags, but only if they are content related. If not, your follower will be disbanded and will stop following you. Boynton's love is amongst the most effective hashtags on Instagram, but I wouldn't make much sense using it. Impulses that don't relate to love try to use less generic and more specific hashtags. You can segment your content using hashtags that are related only to you.

Remember not to include spaces or special characters. Members are allowed. You can use acceptable letters at the beginning of Ishwar to make the hashtag easier. To understand why the top touted and the special characters hashtag with the characters are better than Roman. Letters don't position themselves optimally. This one's with emojis dome position. Well, either keep your hashtag short and easy to remember. A white offensive words give somewhere Arati to your hashtags too. Don't just use the same hashtag all the time as you won't miss the chance to be found through other labels.

Keep in mind that poses should be public so that users can fund them more easily. You touch text on your Instagram stories too, so they have a greater reach. Remember, you don't have to highlight hashtags to make them work. You can place them at the end of the post or whatever you prefer.

Writing Captions

Knowing how to tell a story through a caption is Whitall, and that will help you a lot in your strategy to create a caption that has a huge hook with your followers. It's a powerful tool that is available to all influencers and also limitations will reside in creativity. You decide to have a look at two examples of brands that have managed to slip into the mind and the heart of the consumer. Coca-Cola. And they don't sell you their product. They sell you how you feel when using it.

Users are tired of being sold a product, but they love purchasing emotions. Your followers may forget what you say, but they will never forget how you make them feel. That is why telling us stories through a post has become the holy grail of the great brands that even influencers. Today, Instagram's new organism, Phaedrus, poses to generate engagement and therefore a pulse. They receive a lot of likes, and the comments will be more likely to reach a larger audience than a post that doesn't call for your followers to participate.

Forrester Research claimed that Instagram is the king of social interaction. That is because the most influential brands are registering high rates of engagement. They get two points, three percent interaction for every follower, and this figure exceeded engagement generated by the same brand on Facebook and Twitter. Read a caption and make you fall in love. Instagram is synonymous with giving a little wink to tell your community that you are there. So dear a human being behind your profile.

The tax is essential in this channel for several reasons. You will keep the flame alive between you and your community.

You will make it clear that you are interested in what your followers think of you. And the Texas ideal for reading questions or encouraging participation by writing a caption that gives a full attention of followers also has a creative and intelligible process. To be effective, you must identify the tone of which you want to communicate, identify with quality and on the values you want to be remembered. Be consistent. Make the right combination of major captions. Both things must be connected because you call your pulse.

Have a decent picture. Still, if it doesn't have a good caption or an engaging star in the caption, then you will not generate the reaction you want so much to tell a story. Storytelling is an art of connecting with your audience through stories you need to generate a closeness. So the embassy established a special connection with a studio master for writing good Instagram captions to tell the story behind the image. What should be the beginning of the first word on Instagram ? Only show your followers the first two lines of your caption. So if you want to make sure you don't fall in love, you must see the most essential things in the first two lines. So your followers want to read more, take your time, don't write.

Anything is done in a hurry now if you want to, not if you want to engage our community. Choose their words carefully, be concise, make a call to action. One of the critical points of the caption is to generate interaction. So making a call to action will invite your follower to interact with you, give your feedback, and then even if you are part of something using emojis, not everything is formal and then you can make a good caption. And to use emojis if necessary, just remember and must be promptly. You do not want to bore the audience with a text full of happy faces.

Don't forget to say thank you. If you are collaborating with another influencer brand, it must be not only a label, but also mentioned in the caption. This will generate interest from your followers and generate traffic to your profiles. The first step in writing a proper caption on Instagram is to know your audience and understand what they are looking for in you.

The art of storytelling and social networking has grown so exponentially that today a group of influencer caption influencers has been born whose taste is two turns our caption into a condo blog where they tell their experience, tell their stories, contribute their criticism, and even some uses as a journal or diary. This makes Instagram a perfect social network for microblogging. The magic of caption influencers is to be able to caption with a photo and to connect correctly with a description which works perfectly as a differentiator between so many images accompanied by Walt Disney's 3D.

Analyze Your Audience

On Instagram, nothing happens by accident so soon. Audience analytics, you'll be able to know the demographic of your followers, their age, which content they like the most, and even the hours when they are most active. This will lead you to a plan and to study the content you're going to publish and even the best time you can do it. Just as the companies and brands' massive funds are via person, your duty as an influencer is to find a community that feels an affinity with you that likes your content, and not only that, that is able to interact with it and to share it with other people.

Analyzing Instagram followers is something you should always do if you want to achieve success with your pin, whether you are planning a strategy or not, you need to know what is going on in your social network. But by planning , you can increase your followers' engagement and improve yourself. Then you'll be able to see if your Instagram strategy is achieving its goals. You will soon be able to improve. And they were fun. Your plan to improve your statistics again, still not clear. Well, it's great to know that you always have a dashboard ahead to see what's working, what is not, and what needs to be done to fix it.

Analyzing your followers on Instagram is a part of managing your online community, knowing what is following you and why it's imperative to your brand. So analyzing and measuring should be a core activity within your entire social media strategy. This is essential for several reasons. No one allows you to adopt, adapt your content strategy according to your followers, nor to know the best times of day to share content necessary to notice which of our followers are active and which are not to be able to react reactively to passive once number four. No. What kind of content in your community creators who get an idea of what's the best number five segment your audience better to adapt your strategy to each one.

Number six, analyze what people follow or unfollow you. The answer is simple. By analyzing Instagram's profile metric, the few metrics you need to pay attention to. Number one is the growth rate of followers. If you consider it a social network, a platform for social interaction is clear that this metric would not be the most important of all, but it will be beneficial to control the evolution of the numbers of followers. And this also is not a detriment. It will give you a good idea of how effective your strategy is being funded. The relationship between the action you take and the increase or decrease of your followers is objective at this metric.

Once you upload an image, analyze Wahabis and ask yourself how have my followers increased? What content have you published when too many have decided to stop following you? The famous engagement, the engagement of a publication is the number of interaction ecology, whether they are, they are clicks, likes or shares. This will be a clear indication of the quality of your content on Instagram.

This metric is essential to set a direction of your strategy because it gives a good amount of what your followers like the best. But looking at each publishing format separately, images, videos or stories, you will find it much easier to determine which one works. The best number for audience metrics, Of course. What is going on? Followers. There are several specific metrics. These are the ones that will help you better and determine which your followers are like and what your habits are and how they behave with your boxes.

This allows you to know what your audience is like in terms of demographics and what the peak hours are. Further, the power of our stories is Instagram's most successful too, because they came out into the world. It also has a mattress that can help, you know, if the stories you share are pulling or being well received by your fans. So five metrics are next. The number of times a user reads your story and clicks on the right side of the screen to move to the next story back. The number of times that users see your stories and click on our life or the screen to see again.

Next story, the number of times people switch to see the stories on the following account. This indicates that your stories are not being attractive. Drop Offs the number of times the users and drop out of stories by returning to the feed or as it is, directly responding. This is how many users have direct response to your story. For example, if you are linked to something, how many users are YPO?

Connect with Influencers

Networking is essential, especially if you are looking to meet people in your niche or with a similar audience, working with other influencers can be a great thing, especially if you're out there in the same industry. Today is no longer a question of who can establish more partnership, but of who is capable of doing the hard work. This is why Instagram provides you with the tools that I seek for humanisation, a network inhabited by real communities, by people who support each other and work in teams.

You can establish a network of contacts within the target. You have decided to focus on people who do the same and you and who Of course, are willing to collaborate with you to attend the ones who are the influencers present and where you can make yourself known to make it part of your work. Recognizing the events is also an opportunity for brands to discover their new allies. But does that mean you should only collaborate with the people who are just like, you know, if your business network is made up exclusively of people exactly like you, you won't be missing out on significant business opportunities.

As an influencer, you will have a Conlon's opportunity to collaborate creativity with people in other industries, the benefits of making collaboration with other influencers, aka how you get a brand, the partisan partnership and the generative business opportunities. It will help you to give visibility to your content and therefore aware a weekend of interests of a new audience is an awesome opportunity to make new suppliers or brands interested in you improve your level of communication and other professional skills, such as the leadership will be able to see and meet your company competition, even from ALIETTE allies, whether you want to increase your self esteem and the self-confidence you've all learned about success stories of the past they went through to get to the top.

You'll all be aware of the market trends if you want to expand your professional and digital network, creating alliances can make you extremely far away from how to connect with other influencers. Sync carefully who you want to reach and why not. Every influencer may be suitable to your niche style or goals. If you're contacting influencers in the same niche as yours, they have seen your content, which will make the conversation easier. On the other hand, contacting influencer URL sites or Netsch for areas of interest can have several benefits, such as recommending each other for different areas of interest.

You can't use a server on two, such as hyp auditors and influence city to the reach of the influencer. You wish for Copac. Consider what you want from them and what can you offer to them in return? Sing about the ways in which you and other influencers can work together if you can reach out to them in person. Attend the same event as a book, a personal appointment if necessary. There is something special about a face to face communication and then come next to a that cannot be replaced and then you can use it in your favor.

If you have to resort to digital communication, remember that you are talking to another human being on the other side of the screen. Be kind and allow yourself to reduce the formality since they might generate distance between you and the influencer.

Interact with Followers

Creating content on Instagram isn't about uploading a post and sitting around waiting for millions of likes and comments that down to you, on the contrary, the biggest influencers on this social network take their work so seriously that once they uploaded a post, they take the time to respond to some of their followers comments at the end. And they must be your role models. This is what commitment is all about, calling for action and interacting when people are right to interact with their followers.

Interaction makes the audience feel special. Part of the community. Besides, Instagram has tools that allow you to showcase part of your day to day life and then generate the interaction through questions or surveys on Instagram. Organism does not reward an account full of likes and comments, but those who take the time to respond to your followers and to generate positive feedback from them. Remember, they are not just followers, they are a community and the usual value and make them feel like they are there. Your Instagram profiles like home and your followers are like your visitors and a good host.

You must take care of your visitors, comfort them, feed them, talk to them and provide them with an unforgettable, unforgettable time. If you don't treat your reserve bell at home, well, they want what they want to visit. Again, the answer is obvious. No one likes to stay in a place where they don't receive proper attention. That's why you should focus on treating your followers well, interacting with them and making them feel like they're in the right place by following you. Interaction isn't just about you in replying to comments or messages. It's about you going to the profile of those following you and leaving comments for even their credit quality content.

Have you thought about all the work that goes into taking the perfect picture? Is it worth it when the reward is solved and likes interaction and new followers? The competition is high on Instagram. But if your content is quality, you will have a guaranteed safe audience. Remember that Instagram is a more human social network every day, so your content should be as original as possible. And if you copy, your followers will notice. And if you want to make it your secure income, then you need to take it seriously. And the messaging equipment, they can produce photos and videos to suit your audience and even get advice from professionals, such as the photographers and the graphic designers who can help you create a video appealing content.

Be creative. You remember that interaction is not just about us sitting back and waiting for likes and comments. It must also provoke the interaction by being creative with the creation of content and Of course, by calling for action. Always ask your followers, was it a cincher?

Would you like to see more similar content or even take advantage of the use of stickers in your stories such as the Salathe question? Those questions are a way to generate interaction and at the same time create content almost instantly. As in all social networks, you must interact with the people you are interested in being followed.

Contact Brands

There's no specific a number of followers that determine when you are ready for a brand to contact you, it never hurts to take the risk of taking the first step, a cumbia influence or a micro influence or the goal for brands is assigning exposure, content creation and Of course, generate a sales or traffic bahu say that the brands should strictly make the first contact. It's not something, Strich. If you feel confident about your community, you can offer brand collaboration with Zeil.

After all, there's nothing to lose by trying to do your research before you'll make the first contact with a brand you should do some research about and look at our social network and find the most appropriate way to contact them. Remember that if you want to gain visibility as a professional, you must locate an email that the brand has for the marketing department or for a smaller or emerging brand. Contact them directly. Where was that? If you send a message to your Instagram mailbox, chances are your message will be lost. You want all the attention to be directed to you, even though it's a lot.

The treatment will be as a human, as personalized as possible. Research also gives you the chance to learn about the brand and perhaps identify the critical point where you may be needed. If in your first contact you tell the brand why they need you and it will be easier for them to understand why you will have several points in your favor. You must also take care of a coherence where you have the purpose of contacting a brand that you look for funding. They interact with the arousing interest in you in the same way you have in it.

Money flows into the area of asking for collaboration with brands they do not know. Don't do it to fund the brands that you can identify with and then you think will make your audience fall in love with a good influencer, who knows its audience as not that evil. Like what a sext. You only have one chance to make a first impression. So the brand, they can trust you. And because you went further from the beginning, contact the brands once you have done your research. And the next step is to contact the brand.

Take your time to read a clear and precise message and tell the brand your interest in establishing an alliance. And the collaboration tells them who you are, what your men now are, and the channels that you use to reach your audience. And remember that it's all about honestly selling your image to awaken the brand's interest in you. Also, to the language of the previous research, you did indicate your strengths that others stand out and make the brand want to work with you is not about pointing out the brand and showing that there is something wrong with it, but rather highlighting the attributes you possess that may be relevant to the brand.

Present yourself as a professional. Writing data is essential to justify the investment, the brand that we'll make in the collaboration. If your Instagram account is already a business, our account, you have a statistic to help you get accurate measures of your target audience to read it. Are you sure when they were to be located? And even the most favorable publishing hours data plays a vital role in working with anyone. Look at your disposal, a portfolio of your work or a social media market. This portfolio will not only make you look like a professional from the brand, an advisor can prepare a social media kit. Remember that you don't want to send an email.

Why the job with squishier that you have just made it to your statistic. Professional work must be done in advance to get an Atkeson result and persist without being pushy. There's nothing worse than a pushy, annoying person with an evil brand to give you the first refusal to a proposal you can withdraw after a couple months then reconsidered the offer. In some cases, the brand may indicate it's not the right time or that you can do it later. You're free to propose and they're free to reject is an awesome opportunity to learn. And you don't know the parents that rejected you will be interested in you later. Focus on experience.

Building Your Profile

Even though we talk a lot about Instagram influence marketing, it's not only about Instagram, YouTube, for example, is a social network in recent years that has managed to get a broad audience, a consumer accountant by nature and especially faithful to those who subscribe. Create a YouTube account and build your profile before we get into the depths of the world of video and streaming, you must understand that what is a YouTube as a rapid definition?

You can see that YouTube is a kind of Internet to TV where you can watch what you want and even learn about topics that you never imagined, which also includes live broadcasts. The term television, although now usually used by YouTube, comes to mind because of the increasingly strong integration with the traditional television through smart TV and external devices with Internet assets that connected to a traditional TV allow you to integrate YouTube as if it were just another TV channel. However, today the trend of dozens of YouTube videos is so abysmal that it has overcome the digital barriers and has become a social network.

YouTube as a social network, is now commonly referred to YouTube as the social network. You was a video hosting site on YouTube. Users can interact freely. They can what like and this is really the consumer share videos and the common anthem and the subscribe to another user's channel subscribing be equivalent, for example, to following another user on Instagram, since once they become a subscriber's user will see the news of the channels they have subscribed to every time they enter YouTube. In fact, the number of subscribers, as in other social networks such as Instagram or Tic-Tac, is similar.

Narus with the success is a YouTube channel, just as technical progress has given rise to influential people in various social networks. YouTube is no exception. Millions of influencers to YouTube are to come to life on this social network and that even in the last decade it has become such a profitable profession that the dream of many children of the current generation is to become a great YouTube, as not everything is rosy and not all the professions require a comprehensive knowledge. As in other social networks, you face a larger number of competitors. So the success that you can have will be directly proportional to the experience you have and how you apply it. Like other careers, your success will also depend on the discipline, personal perseverance and the passion you put into it.

What do you need to become a YouTube? The first thing you need to consider is that you don't need a computer or a specific camera, that you don't need to pay attention to detail to generate quality videos. You must try to record your videos using technological research so the first thing you should take into account is that you should do your best. And the university on camera and computers allow you to do a good job as far as your budget allows.

You also need a good camera and minimal editing skills. Don't start a YouTube adventure without basic or technical knowledge, or the results will be weak, poorly valued enough and by the users who follow you remember, that's a matter where almost everything has been done. So you should focus on why your audience didn't have a certain stand up or whatever. You must have a decent camera and the basic notion of audio, video editing and delegate these tasks to some expert in this field. This is because a YouTube video needs video ingredients that engage the audience, such as effects, Futter sticker's and faces.

Nowadays, there are many free storytelling and original narration narration tools at your disposal, a space record. You want to become a gamer, a travel YouTube blogger. But it's a video that you prepare to record in space, looking for proper light conditions and aspects that hinder the quality of the video. Disappear from the screen. A messy room, wrong framing or cool lighting. Give a week and adult results are powerful. The first step is Riversleigh to open the YouTube site, then click on your profile inmate in the top right corner and then you can login. You can do so after operating the same manual. Now, counting the tricky part.

Although my channel options appear in the menu YouTube channel, I'm not created unless you do so manually when you click. There you all be taken to the form of a channel, you also need to enter a first and last name for your YouTube channel. The form fills in the details with those of your Google account and you are free to change them manually. This way you create a channel associated with you as a person if this is what you want. Click on to create a channel if you wish to use a different name than you could use a business or other name. Insert the name you want for your channel, which is what this case does now has to be your real name or press create. The process will create a YouTube channel as well as Google Plus page and the business account for that channel.

You have now created your channel business. Be blunt creating a customizable channel to add your YouTube channel profile and to give you some personality from this page you get at a Hattar Chenda channel image and add a description added in the core elements of your channel. Extremely easy. By leading the mouse over the profile image and cover image, you won't be shown the pencil icon to edit them and upload a new photo you can also write and the channel description. The following is also essential.

A profile picture and a good account picture for the channel. You should keep in mind when designing your M8 that the central blocks of YouTube where oil information appears is six hundred and sixty nine hundred and sixty miles wide. When designing your background image you should not a and it critical elements in that sector because they will remain hidden behind your channel. Another limitation you should consider is that your background image can now weigh more than 250 K.

Just Be Yourself

The most popular YouTube or on the Internet is Swedish police, better known as cutie pie, with over 100 million subscribers and 10 billion with it. He is well, since YouTube or on the planet started in this world by uploading video games where there was no one trendy on the YouTube platform. Yet he did it simply because he was passionate about another unforgettable YouTube success story is Justin Bieber, whose career took off thanks to his popularity on Google smartphone and so on until he achieved his goal this way was discovered while he was still noticeably young through the Sullivans, a reproduction of his videos, performing his songs and nephrons it. It was a production company that started to be interested in him.

The success stories mentioned have reached the top four, making a difference in some personal aspects and knowing how to take advantage of the profession of these young talents. YouTube's is no more than this. Yes, you can earn money and a lot of it by having success with our videos on YouTube to earn money from your content and to gain loyal subscribers over time as a YouTube or uploading any random things along. Suffice to say, you will need to fund your talent and charm and possess some technical knowledge. And we're not about luck to understand both people and numbers to then master the incredibly complex system.

YouTube has become number one, defining the scene of the channel. Content is king without content that people find engaging everyone. No matter how much effort you make at a technical or SEO level. If the content is not attractive, the users will come in once but won't come back. And you don't want that. Your interest must be focused on users who are loyal to the channel, who subscribe and want your content eagerly. That's why, besides making videos with exciting content, you must also take into account the topics and the fun day to reach our target audience. The secret is to be yourself, to find something you like and specifically specify.

For example, you are passionate about makeup. Do you know that millions on YouTube are specialized in this field? And it's almost impossible for you to compete with those who have been in the industry for years and why who are who already have millions of subscribers? And instead of being the YouTube or who doesn't make up tutorials, your channel consists of making anime makeup to do. And then you can be even more specific about doing makeup for a particular anime. You stand out from this one niche initially, but it can be an assonance start.

Discipline and consistency would do the rest. No, to be Bidgemia Bidgemia your ruler who notice right away if you are authentic or not, explore your personality and then show it in your videos by acting just like you do in front of your friends or family, for example, you don't have to copy someone else's stuff, put your passion into it and enjoy nowadays social network focus on humanity. Lateesha. So on YouTube, those for Jinyan are more relevant.

That is to use less to create a character and have a different personality from who you are. Your fans will notice and then you will lose credibility. Besides, honesty is vital if your purpose is to become professional and if later on you want press to take you into account as a criterion influencer.

Set Your Goals

That's all the activities you carried out in your life. If you want to succeed, you must set yourself goals and objectives in the short, medium and long form. The same applies to YouTube, and there are some goals, regardless of your personal goals. And then you should consider YouTube number one, future reputation as a brand, look for an empty market cap and then create valuable content for the people inside YouTube.

Many people do the same, but each one gives it his unique touch. Your main objective should be to Odelay investigating what might be missing that you can provide. Remember, you are a product in the market and you have to fit with your audience. Many YouTube have their brand and they even treat their community as a part of one big family by consuming their content. No, to develop organization and discipline.

Improvisation is useful for some creative endeavors, but part of the success of Big YouTube's conference through planning of their own content is a good idea to limit yourself to one or few particular niches. And talking about that as a starting point, connecting with your audience along the way, you even need to scrape the content that you are going to produce. So that is in the right order. As you shoot a video, you have a beginning, a development, and to not deviate from the center scene, necessarily become a researcher, spend some time researching and going deep into your subject outright. It cannot be a good YouTube or focus on makeup if you don't know the latest and upcoming product. Not a problem. Common Common the channel.

If you do not delve into the latest news and the trends, you have decided to be an educational YouTube, or you will have to take your knowledge and the research and transform it into gagging wives. And we do ASIA that will entertain and educate your audience. If you want to better understand YouTube is otherwise able to take the perspective of a user rather than that of a creator.

Being disciplined and keeping yourself in constant training will help you keep up to date number four and stand your audience. What kind of people are watching you? What do you want to attract? Is not a sin to make a prank for science experiments for children as it is to analyze a French film or to have a channel of other recipes, characteristics such as an age interest, social and economic status, and their behavior in YouTube, a fundamental data that is used online as soon as possible. Number five has a strong presence.

The visual aspect of your YouTube channel is all the most important. It's imperative to take into account the following aspects so that your videos stand out from other YouTube and is the one chosen by the user within the unless upload made are both the title and the cover of a redo will help the users to decide whether to click on the video to play or not. The color should be striking and possible within your corporate image. If you incorporate an image of yourself, we even matter.

The words, including a thumbnail, must be of a significant size to be legible in the small size, a hat keeping the same style for awesomeness and loyalty to your channel and your brand.

Be Consistent

People nowadays say that quality is a thousand times more important than quantity. Over a few realize that quantity is a central part of the strategy when it comes to reaching people in social media. You are going to have high quality workouts, but you won't see the progress if you exercise only once a month. Being all nice and consistent when you start creating content from your channel is essential to your girls on the left.

It doesn't necessarily mean that you have to publish what we do every day. That means that you have to sleep schedule every time you want to upload the new content. This will help you be more organized and keep your audience engaged. Number one, be consistent, maintain a good upload of frequency and be patient with it. YouTube channels don't evolve overnight.

The girl slowly because being seen by people and recommended it takes time. But you also need to consider that to maintain the interest on your channel, frequent updates are necessary. Set a specific day or days during the week so your user base knows what to expect from you and when to come back for more content. If people love your content, you will have them waiting for that. There are days when they're referring to YouTube or making a new upload. If you are starting as a YouTube or there's no need to make overly lindsay.

We do the first 10 seconds of every video, which is crucial, especially as a new YouTube to sell what you offer in that time and don't make too long videos, at least when you're starting to capture an audience. Estimates about the YouTube behavior show that around 80 percent of the users only watch the first ten seconds when skinny for the new count. It is clear that YouTube is not going to bring you much if you don't get visitors. But that's a tough step if you're just starting out in that word. No, YouTube has started with millions of followers.

On the contrary, the process requires a lot of perseverance and a love for what they do. No to be organized, keep a well funded content. The calendar will help you keep publishing content regularly. And then if you choose a topic you like, you can take a notebook with you. And the ride on your smartphone knows the idea to come. Always writing out everything will ensure that no idea is left out. If you are driving ideas and then you are ahead of production, you can always schedule your uploads to go public unless that date and time number three, take care of the space where you make your videos.

Maintaining a space design for your video will help you to give them a particular authenticity to the videos you make. If you don't have ample space, you can use any blank space in your house. Many YouTube videos have started this way. Keeping your space in order allows you to create a video at any time, especially when there is a last minute trend to which you should contribute any criticism or a comment or even an idea you have to document.

Analyze Your Data

Being guided by the numbers of wheels, likes and comments are not enough to know how your YouTube channel is performing. Fortunately, the platform offers detailed performance reports through the YouTube studio to assess. Click on your user icon at the top, right. And you will find the button.

And this is the ideal starting point, as the EP includes easy to understand tables and graphs, as well as a ready-made report. With these resources, you can quickly uncover valuable and meaningful information that you can start working with this the main mattress user review in your digital video channels. No one predicts the success of a video. The first 48 hours of a digital video are crucial. If you get views from 20 percent of your subscribers and mean that you will maintain excellent performers to determine your learn to subscriber ratio, go to create her studio and then compare the number of places to the number of subscribers.

Number two, most popular content to analyze audience participation. Go to Krater studio, go to analytics, tap and select an overview. You will get entire ad graphs of likes, dislikes, comments and shares. You'll also review the performance of the individual windows and identify which one generates the most action. The number three major organic meals, organic traffic. What comes naturally without interruption of paid advertising is essential to know the nature of the video we use to determine how well that YouTube operation works for your channel and whether your video appears in the search results.

In any case, go to the traffic source. You will see at least the figures for each traffic source such as a YouTube search suggests that we use browsing functions number for measuring whizzes through YouTube searches. YouTube is a second. Mostly you. The search engine, mostly users go directly to the platform to make aquarists. These are Mattrick. It's important, especially when your channel is new and little known, since a search engine is particularly the only way to get by. So it's a window to optimize the SC of your video.

Check all these metrics in the traffic source number five, we didn't hire this metric. It's critical to identify whether you are engaging the audience with your content or not. There may be videos with many wheels where users only stay for the first few minutes and then leave in another take like a playback time. In the graph you can see the average waiting time your audience spends on your videos and the list below the time Bricktown for each of them. If you click on any of them, you will see its graph number six retention. Retention is a mattress that helps you determine how relevant to your channel and videos are to the audience.

With this, you will know the average length of stay of the users within your channel. And the key points are for each video where you achieve higher audience retention. If the user wants to watch a scene again, it will slow higher intention at that point. Number seven most recommended video was a traffic source. And you can see the number of times your video up here has been recommended. This is a great way to increase our channel's popularity, especially if your video appears at the suggestion after a popular one.

Come to see which of your videos appear most frequently as recommendations. As you can see, having a large number of subscribers, it's not enough if you discover that they are now watching your videos, but you have not kept you waiting for them with content, a detailed audit to identify patterns on the works best and to optimize your channel.

Contact Brands

Carnley has a ninety one point five billion users per month, roughly 80 countries have users on YouTube who consume an average of one billion hours a day of content every minute. About 400 hours of content are uploaded to YouTube. These data indicate that the video catsuit consumption has been increasing among Internet users. Besides, YouTube is the place where you can find all kinds of content in video format. Therefore, everything indicates that total today YouTube is available to it and a digital marketing strategy. That's why the most prominent brands have their channels mirror.

Addition to creating highly creative content, they form strategy as it is with the most notable YouTube influencer. So what action is right for you? There are different tactics that you can implement with smaller parties, which will depend on the focus of the negotiation. Therefore, you must know some of the different types of strategy you can apply to work together with the brand. Number one, marketing to the brand is a pruners step to formalize a relationship with a brand and include all actions then made to contact you and discuss.

Create a proposal to establish a partnership. It consists of showing the brand why they should ponder and reveal that you must not use Merryville, the market in which your potential allies are located, to understand how to generate value in your proposal. Likewise, it is advisable to include a call to action. After all the presentations of benefits to make them schedule a meeting or pursue a counterproposal many times is also useful to include a PDF document with some reverse action you have done with other brands or even your channel statistics. It should be like a resume, but in this case you should have continuously updated.

Another one is marketing with a brand as the alliance is created. We move on to the making of the video, Of course, reading all the ideas that exist so that in this case the value of the brand gets highlighted, choosing a template that bulls share through social networks. It's a good Predix, so they will be aligned as brands and the seek to generate the impact from the both communities marketing sort of brand with this category is a feat in marketing, where in your role as an influencer is to serve as a bridge, the public exit publicity to the thought or the content of the brand. It's also usually the case where the product is offered with some special discount to the community with a specific code. This way the brand can know how many people you have.

A genius reached marketing for the brand. It's the model modality in which one party uses its positioning and engagement to attract a quality audience. Why is the other party in charge of the follow up? This strategy is applied to then work towards a convergence of those with a basic profile to become users of a brand, stirring the moment of a Perles with strategy. Ideas can be greatly beneficial as long as you know how to do it without being in a position to lose. Within that symbolism generated with working with others, preparing the ground for a conquest, more and more companies are starting to reap the benefits of doing business with others.

So can you dare to create your winning islands, islands and below you will fund a series of criteria that you should be clear about before going down this new path. Number one, define your objectives. You can start looking for allies if you don't know what you need them for. You must first determine where your channel is at because if you are in a girl's face, you will need to urge her more about what you're doing.

Keep in mind that with establishing a new alliance, if your alley is more consolidated in the market, you may give more in the relationship. This does not mean you will lose, or rather that you will be targeting a market that probably does not know the type of service you are offering. Therefore, knowing what your objectives are will give you the guideline of understanding what kind of aliens you might need, which market to target, and what action with a search party might attract new customers to keep the points clear.

As in any relationship, conditions need to be clear from the outset. Each stakeholder must know what the expectation regarding the. Are and what they have to give in return, this helps to maintain harmony and allows you to work more comfortably. Why build that trust that often grows stronger over time. Number three, sooner target. Sharing a common audience to extend is necessary for interested parties because this will complement the offer of post and that action will provide a positive result for all interested parties who are calling MISTA when starting to work together with other brands just because those who manage them are trustworthy people.

Even though each company's market is different, this situation is often short-lived. The losses are directly proportional to the full fatality of efforts to stimulate further revenue due to a lack of consistency in your channel's value proposition. If you want brands to take an interest in you, you must create content that is worth sharing that will spark interest in new audiences. After all, the main objective of brands is to achieve exposure and then reach through your channel.

What It is & How It Works

In the summer of twenty eight. A new app appeared in the social media landscape. When you open it, you can find funny videos with unusual effects and audio created by the users. This new app resembles for most people to win the app that featured a short video that Twitter shot out in 2017. As soon as you enter the app, everything feels random in your comfort way.

The succession of strength we do doesn't seem to follow an algorithm, but it's very entertaining. And even though the videos are less than a minute long on average, it seems like you can spend hours watching. The app is Tic-Tac, but what is ticked off is more than a random collection of funny videos with copyrighted audio tittered application from Beatdowns. A Chinese technology form is a social network with which main feature is the ability to recruit, add it and upload a schroedinger's enhanced with augmented reality of community with ability to add a Baggara audio front is a hybrid library users resist and incorporate a year before Dickason lunch beatdowns board ownership rate of musically app and then converted in what is today with over 500 million active users per month.

To App is a mix of two apps which were groundbreaking back when they were Lunch one and the musical prior to takeoff. Formally appearing musically possesses virtually the same interfaith. The app features the ability to perform lip synching and do collaboration with friends there. When you login to tick tock, you will enter a video time frame similar to the one displayed a musical with a broader variety of video seems from one page to memes to choreograph full of A.R. filters, but always random, which is one of the most outstanding features of this network.

How does Tretyakov work? There is indeed no rocket science behind the operation of this application, but some things can help you understand it a little bit more. For Statter, you don't need to register if you just want to watch a few videos. But if you're going to publish, follow or give like another user, you will need to open an account.

You can do this by signing in with a social media account, Facebook, Twitter or Google accounts by registering with an email or your cell phone number. Once you write down that there's nothing left to do but start exploring it is easy to do. But it's easy to understand if you follow the steps below number one open application and have the plus sign top in the middle tab, the icons surrounding the main recording interface. These will allow you to add audio and the visual effects set a time and a bottom to choose how long your video will last.

Star recording you want to go or in sections. Once you record your raw footage, the test text sticker's effects and music to have next in the following screen you get just your publication settings, just a comment and the privacy settings by touching the buttons for each of the options below the video description window.

Get a Pro Account

If you ever wonder about how to understand the younger generation, think otherwise, I tick-tock because I understand that they use to a T. It might be too fast paced and overwhelming for some, but younger audiences thrive on it. It's no coincidence that 40 percent of its user base is under the 16 to 24 age gap. This curious social network is a phenomenon among young people. However, it has now generated the same hype in mature social network consumers. The reason for that is rather straightforward is because of Ticos intentional design tintypes.

Popularity within the use is explainable by stating that Tuscarora eight are aimed from the very beginning and under 18 demographic sector. In a manner of speaking, it's safe to say that Tip-Top developers took the time to understand the teenager sector by their then competing apps having a clear target from the get go. They have followed the behavior of this age group, closely leading them to develop a social environment that can give a teenager and the youth young adults precisely what they want.

Tick Tock is a space in which users can create and share fun videos featuring some lip synching, singing, dancing to an incredible variety of sorts that enables younger audiences to express themselves creatively. Whether they are doing some kind of comedy or performing art, it's amicable and easy to use social networks. So it's not surprising that more people are drawn every day. That's why by now, millions of celebrities have already created their Tic-Tac accounts. Even the renowned Agim Jimmy

Fallon has previously recorded more than one viral video and also doused the famous and the viral Rajani a challenge together with a gigantic talk Kirt Charlie, the Allama deal known by being the girl who is more followers on the network with only 16 years old, t talk is not going to disappear for a long time.

Although companies like Facebook have tried to recreate that, they haven't come close to insult. Like every social network that takes off on the position itself, Twitter has also decided to offer us what they call a pro account with special tools for content creators. This is very similar to the professional creator, and the business accounts provided by Instagram offers you the possibility to receive your account statistics and the BUJAR strategies under at the moment to talk pro provides us with our account statistics. We can have and manage up to three different accounts. If your goal is to be part of this fantastical viral phenomenon called Tic-Tac, then you should create a pro account to be able to assess the statistics. These are the steps you must follow.

No one, open your account application, go to the party and take you to the profile, then click on the three doors at the top of your screen. When the drawdown menu opens, select a manager account option. At the bottom, you will feel the speech or come pro option. Being pro, you all have tools available, such as statistics. So like the category you wish to belong to, include a phone number or email. You want to receive a message about Esmat apps and or with a four digit code, you include it in your account and then you have a ticker pro account. Once you follow these steps, you will start to see your account statistics, and use them properly with data. You have a significant advantage compared to other social networks. That's a network that is emerging and growing. You can take advantage of the statistics and go far.

Videos You Should Create

If you are interested in joining Ticked for personal or work related reasons, it can always be useful and very entertaining to see the poses either have made and thus inspire you even as they're in all social networks. There's content for everyone, but some highlights, much more emeriti is a taste for your niche and the audience to target and then create a content for the talk, stand out for the ease with which we can be created.

Not all of them are incredibly complex, added. Some are even easier than you think, but which of those formats stand out in time? Some differences are strongly noticeable. First of all, music videos or Wantage. On any given day, you can watch many musical Mondays Erminio meaning home music video on the platform. Although many people generally prefer to lip synching you for others who are more creative.

For example, a trend that younger users love is creating stories in Remould. Using the song as a song plays, the story unfolds. Why? What happens relates to the lyrics perfectly. Number two is physical comedy and meme's. Most of the posts you will see on Ontake. I intended to provoke the reaction with a greater shower of comments and like Lauffer is usually a sudden for that, although you often see some symbols and the funny videos, you will also see some others that are more elaborate. And the Wellbelove in the post with whether Srour Narrative's.

Besides, you offer funny videos with a very specific format or around a set reference or punch line. These are memes which have the advantage of being adaptable to almost any situation as long as their core template is respected. This template is usually a particular audio with a time reaction or predictable ending at the Punchline. Number three, we deal with a specific special effect. Some make use of the hot food or others have become transitioned. Weezer's recently a stream of talkers called a transition or have been derived, and they are showing off their creative skills to create a video with the Laser transition that up here to ordenes, others even create even more elaborate videos with more professional comment kamik than what they decide outside of tea. Talk about shirts. They are and Of course are loved by the users. Tweets are perhaps the most comfortable option to use our platform with it.

You can respond to a musical post by recording your radio with the same music. You can generate a response video to our reaction video or even be more creative. There is no limit to creativity in Tic-Tac challenging videos and I think that you can also see regularly announced challenges with a hashtag. These are videos aimed to motivate you to record yourself doing something weird to draw the challenge. You can usually find them at the bottom of the home screen, right under the magnifying glass where you are having fun . The hashtag was the most popular challenge of the moment tutorial as an honor.

Never many people want to learn how to do things, so making a tutorial of what you can do can be very useful. Every day more and more people share tutorials about how the face must make our food and the secret to do something creatively with your personal touch.

Your Tik Tok Strategy

Now and at first glance, TTR seems to be just the place of random poses, however, its popularity and its user friendly interface they focus on video gives a chance to the brand to conduct a marketing campaign and create opportunities to make their products and the service interesting. This opens up a new niche for influencers and the new possibility with a high probability of success. If you want to stand out in it and be an influencer or tick talker, you must manage a strategy.

No. One interacts with your audience as in other social networks. Your interaction with other net people, not robust. So you must make interaction with your followers a fundamental part of your life on this platform. So this way your audience will feel loved and relevant. You can ask them a question or survey or recommend them for others to visit their profile. Remember that here the relationship is reciprocal. They need you as much as you need the number to produce quality content. It seemed like it goes without saying, but you need to remember all your content and the marketing efforts, whether they are targeted or not, should be supported by an appropriate strategy that seek to add value to your audience, even if you only want to entertain them right away, sing about what you are and leaving your readers one more ad spam or whatever make it worthwhile to follow you and not others.

The nursery post, frequently both quality and quantity, are important. If you wish to be successful in your niche, you have to make your community understand that you are a reliable entertainer, an active creator. The best way to do that is by posting frequently. However, there's no standard to determine the right frequency of posting. You can do it as many times as you want, but during the day it's more important to upload one quality video a day than temporal quality videos. Number four, get to know your competition to New York direct competition. You must focus on a specific niche. Once you define the funny, you will be able to understand who to target. And Of course, who had the same target audience as you. Don't be shy. You can always do a video response or do it with your competitors and get yourself known in the process.

Number five, learn from other influencers on tick tock, learning from those who are already succeeding and growing in this network. It's not a bad thing. You can even take some of them for inspiration and react to your videos. You have all your creativity available to gain inspiration and do things your way.

No.6 knows your audience. Don't post for the sake of hosting research with your audience and then give them what they asked for. Which also applies, Of course, to hashtags, specialize and take advantage of your beach. Eventually you will be able to add your hashtags or challenges and then your audience will ritualize up.

Getting More Followers

With more than 80 million monthly searches on Google, you can say that is a real Jagannath comparable to Facebook, whose presence is increasingly massively every day, Tetum managed to position itself as a most a download app in the word and the beginning of 2020 when they achieved a nearly 16 million installation, of which the most substantial portion comes from India, followed by the United States, similar to honor.

Social media hashtags talk about social media because they allow you the information and the conversation topics. Also, you can search for hashtags directly in the act of search engine, along with a specific user's in the. The primary function of a hashtag is to target specific content so users can search for it and the funding more easily. So if you want to spread your product or facilitator's viral there, you can use a hashtag so the user can more easily reach her website. What else is a hashtag to increase our followers because they increase the digital word of mouth to help you find your compact competition. Because when you click on the hashtag you use, you can see who else is using it so you can rescind or strengthen your marketing efforts. They make your product more visible because they have restrengthened your branding and the visibility team. So better use the hashtags, use content, the hashtags. This one is very simple.

A common is one that is in the schedule, a part of a campaign. But simply describe what a post contains. That's why it is called that. For example, if you use cosplay and make videos related to anime, the cosplay or cosplay player will be perfect for you to label your accountant. Something as simple as this can help you position yourself better to your ideal audience member to create or participate in challenges. While much of the detail, the content is music related and the reality is that most people use a tool for comedy and to show off their challenges. So you can create one. And Of course, don't forget to tag it with the right hashtags necessary.

Get on the trending topics, the hashtag you get in the magnifying glass. Otherwise they are more entrenched. If you want to take off, you can take advantage of them, make videos with content related to the hashtag trend and to take the advantage of the wire on that. Number four, create a catchy hashtag for inspiration. Search for your video on other networks such as Facebook, Instagram or Twitter before implementing. If it turns out that your idea is super common, you are in time to change it. Number five, keep it simple. Hashtags are easy to write and pronounce.

Srour and the straightforward forward. Do not put some words that you cannot pronounce so it can be shared more easily. Recommends that the public also value minimalism and simplicity. So most popular hashtags will leave you with a list of the most popular hashtags at a time of the writing tick top mean challenge to challenge love. Cute follow fun and the music for your page. Those are very popular.

Followers Hack : Challenges

If you want to laugh for a while and test your nation, there's nothing like that challenge. These are fun challenges turned to the Internet and have us trying things we never saw us to do. If you're looking to succeed in 2000 and succeeding in one of their Wirral challenges might be a good angle, although we warned you, you will have to practice a lot because it's not so easy to get it right the first time. Do you care to try? How do you do challenges in your favor? There are two ways in which you can approach challenges. Starting a challenge or drawing one.

Starting your own challenge when done properly can come from work order interaction generated into followers. For you, however, you need an interesting premise or help from your community to visualize it. Therefore, starting to challenge becomes considerably easier and the more established you are as a tick talker. On the other hand, you gain a lot of visibility by participating in an already established challenge. Depending on your performance on camera and with the help of your differentiators animate, you can gain a high amount of interaction. And the followers, some examples of challengers.

Currently, Charlie DeMello is the most popular girl in Tick-Tock, with almost 60 million followers on the platform in less than a year. The girl went from being a 15 year old girl from Connecticut to being perhaps the most famous face of the Z generation in the United States. And sooner or later, globally, Charlie became famous for her choreography and the style to dance. Her most notable hit was a Carol Gaffing Redit

Originate, a song turned into a meme. After that, she joined the Los Angeles take to hip hop collective.

As if this wasn't enough, she became the first influencer to star in a Super Bowl commercial. Her popularity was so overwhelming that the other top stars began inviting her to collaborate and work together. These regional Regenhard challenges became Wirral, which made her a star. But it's not all about dancing. There are some super simple and fun challenges. There are not only Perfidia for attracting an audience and entertaining them, but also for having a good time in the company of your family and friends.

The winner is the loser. These activity companies are turning your back to the camera then together with your friend and then you must activate the following faces: Futter to turn to the or the music to discover who is the first to be focused and affected. This lucky person will be the loser and must serve a punishment. A set at the beginning of this video. Or even if you want to make it even more interactive, you can designate the challenge to the followers. One strategy used by some tutorials to set a challenge to the comment.

The winds are most likely, and in this way the call to action is implicit and it becomes a fun task for both Widowmaker and the viewer. There is even more to serve as an example as it is the real challenge. This is one. The most critical challenge of two topics is that we do not seek to entertain for a while, but to start a conversation with the consequences of bullying in our lives and the importance of stopping with a real challenge. Several content creators have told us their experience with bully stories. Makir makes us think twice about our actions and the repercussions that we have on the lives of others.

Post Frequently

Osos idea we used to have is that tick tock is a network exclusively for teenagers, nothing could be further from the truth, although this platform started by Luke cooking the little ones with their dances and was a musical in the last months, young people and adults have been drawn to it and they see in this social network and you vocal to get their messages to millions of people. We already fund surgeons, psychologists, marketing specialists, designers, nutritionists, sportsmen and women who take it very seriously and the sheer quantity, educational content. This is necessary to emphasize that tick tock is a social network where morality is just around the corner and that everyone has many or few followers, and has the equal opportunities to appear on the four page attack.

Attracting the public will always be the objective of the users. However, to do so there must be an indispensable ingredient. Consistency. This never mostly inhabited children and teenagers is becoming very popular among adults who are also trying to find a space on the net. However, some are harshly criticized because they seek to do the same thing that children who have already acquired a popularity have been doing. If you're an adult, you don't necessarily have to do the same thing that kids do.

You can play with your creativity and make videos that, Of course, are attractive but always try to adapt them to Europe. The key to success in data is to be true to yourself. And then consistency is what allows you to stay in the minds of your followers and not have your content lost over time. This one who likes what you do will be faithful to you and help you grow. Or people produce a series of sensation when you see them for the first time. That initial sensation is what will give you one position or another in the minds of the users.

A clear example is of this is the first time we see someone that first impression we get a general idea of that person, because what we have received, the image of a profile versus same way, don't be afraid to be funny, but responsible coherence and the consistency of the fundamental pillars on which your brand must be built, what you are, and the mark you want to leave on the work. This is a way to differentiate yourself from the competition and get closer to your desire to target an audience. You have rights, but you also have obligations.

Someday we will inherit not only DAPS or properties, but we will also have the opportunity to inherit our knackwurst profiles. All that information that over the years we have uploaded, commented on the contacts. We made an essential source of data for our here and the way we did business with whom and what it deforms. How you are holding out in social networks as an influencer. Are you aware that you are an opinion leader?

How big data is generated from the first day you use the internet and social media is a quantity you are producing is what can be critical. Tay's for something, your work, your Trex insurance and your lifestyle. And in ways of thinking being consistent, it can even be your most prominent attraction for brands. Because Serabee is consistent between what you say and what you do, and that in the long term is beneficial to work together with others.

Using Tik Tok Analytics

The first step to start understanding analytical data is to know how to assess it from your production in this app. Just follow these steps to do so, switch to the parole account from your profile. Click on this report on the top. Right. And go to the manager, Kang Mannu. You often in the lower part of the option, highlighted with a blue letter say switch to payroll account.

The information will start to register right after you have switched to the account and it might take up to seven days to begin showing the different insights. During this time, they are able to post as much as possible to collect more information after starting to see the first numbers in this section of the application. Now comes to the point that all systems should understand the analytical data and tick the adequate data and think that the information in this statistical section is divided into three key sections. The first one is Profar overview.

The second one is fun insights. An assertive one is called an insight general provided at the first national database. And I think the data is particularly useful to know how the overall performance of the account is here. You can see the information from three critical sections of your profile. The first section is a number of the views, which the number of times the detailed content was revealed within seven to twenty eight days. The information in this section appears by day. The second section is a powerful real, a metric that indicates how many times the top or profile was revealed, also within seven to twenty eight days.

The information is also presented by day. And because of this you can see what content is bringing people to your profile. Finally, the sort of section of this first section is a follower account. From this, a graph shows how the numbers also evolve in a period of seven to twenty eight days by concerning this number. And it's the evolution through the days you call line the population of content to determine which was the most attractive ones to the point of motivating the app's user to follow your account follower and site under the sentence. Second, sexuality does anatomical data. Things are more straightforward. The platform displays a demographic of the people who follow your account.

Considering the gender and the region from which they see you here it is possible to encounter all kinds of countries because of scale and which platform works. Moreover, the data shown also covers a period that can go from seven to twenty eight days. Although a minus seems so important to have this information, you should know that it can also be an excellent guide for the company. You will develop for the platform brands that want to captivate more people in certain regions can take this data into account and know if direction has the expected effect content then. Finally, the analytical data section on data offers window information divided into several sections designed to better understand the results you're getting.

In the first instance, is it possible to see the total number of publications launched in a period of seven to twenty days and the number of reproductions revealed that they achieved at that time? The polls are shown from the oldest to the most recent. Just below this first section either trim the section of trending which reviews which we do have been popular in your account during that period. It's also possible to see the number of plays obtained within this section. Each of the videos have more data to show. This is one of the most useful features, autodidacts and any good data. If you click on any of the videos shown in the section, more information will be displayed, such as the number of likes obtained.

A number of comments or shares by the data is also possible to see the total playback time of the content, the total place, average playback time, the type of traffic sources and the region of the audience. As with other platforms, this information helps the just published content to increase shows and matches or determine if what is being published is effective. As you can see, the top is serious and you are already a little tired. All the social networks keep an eye on this platform in case it ends up replacing Instagram in the future. However, everything possible is run, including all top features Rowsell.

When to Contact Brands

It's a social network that is still in an emerging state, makes all brands, and we also have a presence there that is in the eye of many brands that want to increase their reach. And right now, top is among the best ways to do it than by taking advantage of their trend. After all, if there's a lesson to be learned from Twitter, is that taking risks beyond a traditional skin and trusting creative endeavor can help you earn the loyalty of your followers. And that triggered lots of attention to worship there, as in the app. But they are not invasive. And the major brands such as Huawei, Samsung, Apple, Shell, me and Opal are directly involved with the technology development for this app.

The big production companies, owners of songs, songs and movies allow the use of their content on the platform. Each audio or subsequence is played by billions and billions upon when used by people manning that brand exposure, especially in the entertainment market. This makes it a multi-million dollar social network without the need to invade a feed with advertising because it does not allow the links to publications and until recently started allowing advertising these businesses focus on the visibility that a platform can give them and not a tool that ensures them to gain new customers to succeed in time.

You must be extremely creative, especially if you want brands to look at you as a fundamental part of the community. Wunderkinder a brand as in other social networks, quantity is substantial. And the quality is even more so to understand when the right time is, you must look at your statistics and to work on a strategy. If you don't have a direction, you will know where to go once you have your strategy. You have to create a highly creative, confident attitude that can catapult you to success. These can be done by an expert marketer or publicist who can guide you based on what strategy you can work if you are yourself in the or knowledge to your advantage. Growing up will be easy. Another fundamental point that you must take into account is that your video must generate impressions. That is to say, Commentaries and sharing are not just a shower of likes.

Make calls to action within videos or with a short, concise caption that gets your follower to comment. Once you consider you have the Raimo in your account that you will be able to reach out to others, then you will be able to contact brands that you think can be identified with zeal or whose values are in line with yours. Don't forget that for this you must already have a well established target audience, a well-defined niche and explosive creativity. How do you corral this process? The first step, as always, is to identify brands that may be interested in your niche and they can address your audience, such as a case of some talkers who do tutorials on photo editing applications and applications like Picasso, like giving them a whole year of their code or pro working.

Once you identify the brands, you must contact them. It is not always a brand to have to continue to do this. Make your social media kit available to the brand where you not only include your information and the statistics from Tector, but from all the social networks you are present. Create a personalized email and let them know you are interested in working with them. Take care of your message and the spelling. Try to write a concise message that summarizes your information and why they work with you. This is fundamental. That will increase the interest of the brand. And you include photos and some links to you, most of the relevant content.

And Of course tell them how they can contact you if they become interested in your proposal, show the brand why they need you and why your presence at the top can be done to them. Remember that your interests. Brands are more interested in those who are not a copy paste of others. Try to personalize your message, study the brand and talk directly to them.

Conclusion

We live in the digital age where technology advances by leaps and bounds, where one day something might be part of the trend and the new one overtakes the next day to Newroz, created by this digital revolution, seems to be here to stay. And this is not something that can be predicted because two or three decades ago, nobody would have imagined that television, radio and traditional advertising would become obsolete. However, as long as the opportunity is this, this is a must to be used to the food. There are already millions of brands that every day decide to work together with.

The influencers who make life in many social networks that exist might even make it their profession and their full time job because they can take it very seriously and then work tirelessly to generate enormous profits. And all those social networks have led us in digital trust to send this. The primary purpose of these will always be for people to be more social. It's all about humor, interacting with other humans. You must take into account that if you want to become an influencer, you must prepare yourself because technology advances and you don't want to be left behind. It doesn't matter if you are a celebrity, an influencer or a micro influencer.

The goal will always be the same to grow and offer brands the many advantages of influencer marketing by working with you and thus boosting their cells while increasing their reach and exposure in influencer marketing. However, it's not a quantity, but the percentage of interaction engagement to your publications generally that is important. Get your values right, find something you like and identify a good niche for yourself, for your audience and the content for them. Also, define your objectives. Be very clear about what you want to achieve because it will help you not to deviate from your long term goal to now work within a strategy.

Influencer marketing is a surprisingly effective technique that even though it remains a mystery for a considerable portion of the market and can be undoubtedly risky, those who have decided to take the risks have succeeded in terms of earning money, reputation and convergence. Therefore, if you want to awaken their interest, a strategy that leads you to achieve long and medium term objectives will be the key to your success. Be honest and forthright with the brands. One of the main advantages of this measure is that unlike its traditional marketing, you have a leverage to negotiate directly with the brand how the campaign is going to be made.

Parents will trust your expertise in your areas of influence because as an opinion leader in Netsch, who is better than you to determine how to reach your community, such an organization generates results in win-win strategies. They will grant you more attention from the brands and earn you more money and success and to finally put love and passion into what you do. It's not worth doing something just because it's trendy or because you want to make money.

The secret of many YouTube or Instagram or even tick talkers who have achieved fame today is that they do not make videos for work. They do it because they want fun. The fund is an activity that they enjoy doing, a job you like, and then you will have to work a single day in your life.

www.ingramcontent.com/pod-product-compliance
Lightning Source LLC
Chambersburg PA
CBHW070117230526
45472CB00004B/1303